TRI-CHEVY

TRI-CHEVY

THAT MEANS '55, '56 AND '57 CHEVROLETS

MIKE KEY

Osprey Colour Series

First published in 1985 by Osprey Publishing
59 Grosvenor Street, London W1X 9DA
First reprint spring 1986
Second reprint autumn 1987
Third reprint autumn 1988
Fourth reprint summer 1989

British Library Cataloguing in Publication Data

Tri-chevy: that means '55, '56 and '57 Chevrolets.
—(Osprey colour series)
1. Corvette automobile—History
I. Title
629.2'222   TL215.C6
ISBN 0-85045-615-0

Editor Tim Parker
Design Gwyn Lewis
Printed in Italy

First page It's easy to identify the different years of tail
lights. Picture line up goes '55, '56 and '57 at the end

Title spread Dale Egle sneaks his '57 210 Delray Club
Coupe, named *Poison Ivy*, over the crest of a hill into the
Classic Chevy Club's convention held in Columbus, Ohio.
   This car was an award winner, and rightly so. It took
three and a half years to complete although the car is not
of the all original breed, running a Chevrolet 327 cu.in.
engine, finely detailed as is the Turbo 350 auto gearbox
to a stock rear axle. Most notable front changes are the
tube grille, shaved hood, and filled front fender louvers.
Paint is candy apple organic green over black pearl
lacquer. The paint is topped off with a super green
pinstriping job. Dale just had to make a neat job of this
car as it was a 1957 Dealer Demo car

Right See how your identification of years is – '55, '56
Wagon, '56 Sports Coupe, '57, '55 Wagon, front line. '57
Convertible, '57 Bel Air Sports Coupe, '57 Sports Coupe,
'55, second row. '57 *Big Bopper*, '57, '57, '55, '55 rear,
and '56 Nomad at the back. If I am wrong, don't tell me.
Just part of the parking lot at the Hilton, Columbus, Ohio

Contents

Introduction

Tri-Chevy, the good years. I was most pleased when Osprey Publishing asked me to assemble a book on '55, '56, '57 Chevrolets, called *Tri-Chevy*. Next, to my first love of street rodding, classic Chevrolets of these three years rate high in my world of cars. Although I own a 1932 Ford, a '40 Chevrolet, a '40 Plymouth Coupe and my wife owns a VW Sedan Delivery at this present time, we have not had the opportunity to own a Tri-Chevy. I have always liked to get close to the large annual display of them at the British Nationals held at Knebworth Park, to talk to the owners, both guys and gals, may I say, of the British TriChevy Club.

With thoughts of collecting some photographs of British Tri-Chevys, I organised a small meeting near to my home in Norfolk. We all had an enjoyable day, I shot some nice photographs and some are included in this book. Thanks to the TriChevy Club. Maybe one day I will own one and become a member of your club.

As Tri-Chevys are pretty rare in England, we packed our bags and flew off to Columbus, Ohio, USA to attend a Classic Chevy Convention. This is where the rest of the photographs were taken thanks to the Classic Chevy Club and all the members and owners we met.

It all started in 1955 with models ranging from one fifty, two tens and Bel Airs. Chevrolet also introduced a V8 engine of 265 cu.in. capacity. It has been a very successful engine; not only was it installed in Chevrolet

production cars in '56 and '57 but is right up to present times in the form of the 283 cu.in., 327 cu.in., and 350 cu.in. These engines have been transplanted into street rods (I have a 327 in my '32 Ford and a 350 in my '40 Chevrolet), dragsters, roundy-roundy cars (*NASCAR* even), Volkswagens, vans, two and three wheel motorcycles, tractor pullers, pick-up trucks; the list is endless.

Tri-Chevys have also been used as themselves classics and featured in many films. A '55 was used in *Two Lane Blacktop* and *American Graffiti*, for example. Tim Cooke featured in an English film called *Shutdown* with a '57 owned at the time by Tony Vandetutte, recently purchased from Keith Harvie. Tim also owns a hot '55 Chevrolet with a big block Chevy.

For *Two Lane Blacktop* Richard Ruth built two identical '55 Chevys with a third for a crash scene; each of the three cars were outfitted with 454 cu.in. engines. The two main cars were heavily modified in the front chassis with a tube front axle on Koni shocks. The engines were equipped with all the goodies, the cars were painted in grey primer and the story line of the film was of two guys drag racing the car across America; the crash scene was never done for the film.

After a good thrashing in *Blacktop* the two lead cars were made into one hot '55 for *Graffiti*. The third stunt car was used in the crash scene at the end of that film but a junker was used to set on fire.

These were hot Chevys; just before they

were handed over to the film company, they
were timed on at a drag strip at 10.90, at 127
mph.

I hope you all enjoy this book as much as I
have taking the photos and fitting the captions
to them. Over the past few months I have
learnt a lot on Tris. If you want a more
historical or technical background read a book
by Pat Chappell called *The Hot One*. I would
like to thank all the people who have helped –
Harry Sunderland and Chris Boyle for note
taking, the TriChevy Club in England, the
Classic Chevy Club of America and their
president Doug Moorhead, and my wife June
who has to put up with it all.

Remember Bel Air in French means
'beautiful line'.

Mike Key
January 1985

This book is dedicated to my two children,
Rachel and Matthew (who took the photograph
on the right), both have great love for
Tri-Chevys.

Gallery of ten custom cars

Black 'n Candy '55

First thing that strikes you about Larry Fullerton's 1955 Hard Top is the candy paint over the black lacquer. Candy paint like this was a big thing a few years back and it is nice to see a '55 with such paint still around. It was painted by Harvey Scott. The car was brought back from California by a friend of Larry's and the original cost was $500, not as much as the 1955 price of around $2000. Larry has owned the car since 1968 and has owned two other '55s.

We have a hint of what is under the hood with the external rev counter and scoop for more air and clearance. To clean up the front the badge and hood bird have been removed, as has the stainless vertical trim just

past the door pillar. Larry is a truck driver who likes to drag race his '55. The basis of the engine is a Chevy small block, 302 cu.in. with a Racer Brown roller cam and a pair of Chevy 202 heads. To pump the gas in he installed a Weiand Tunnel Ram inlet manifold and to top this off, two Holley 660s, hence the hood scoop.

The whole engine and bay is finished with lots of chrome and stainless braided lines, Mallory Msd ignition lights the gas and Hooker headers help get rid of it. All this horsepower is passed through a Doug Nash five-speed manual gearbox, through a 'strange' driveshaft to a Dana 60 axle

Above Fine stance; Firestone slicks on Cragar chrome wheels, biggies on the rear and skinnies on the front, in the true drag racing style

Left Black diamond pleated interior was sewn up by Ambassador House in traditional hot rod theme. The stock dash has more gauges than the original, all relating to monitor the engine internals when drag racing; the stock steering wheel was swapped for that from a Chevrolet Impala

Fine '55

Above It takes a second look to see how Fine Ralph Soto's '55 Bel Air is — it's just black! It sits super on those highly polished Weld wheels and Pro Trac tyres. To aid the 'just off' level stance, one coil was cut from the front springs to lower the front suspension. Stock body with stock trim and that oh-so deep black paint by Don Jeffers

Right The giveaway to something special under the hood is the air scoop. Heart of this pounder is a 350 cu.in. small block Chevy with 30/30 cam and 2.02 heads. Offenhauser inlet manifold has a Dyer supercharger, highly polished with two 750 Carter carbs, Hooker headers complete the set-up. A Muncie M21 gearbox puts the horses through to the stock rear axle with 4:11 ratio

Right We were looking for something 'wild' to feature and Dan Marshall's '55 Sedan Delivery really fills this bill. The top was chopped, the one piece tilt hood has a Corvette grill and twin canted headlamps

Bottom Ralph also told us that all the suspension parts are chromed, born out by the chromed rear axle.
A full set of Sun gauges are installed in the dash, and '76 Grand Prix bucket seats in black velour were installed for more comfort, and a late model Corvette steering wheel keeps this '55 on the straight and narrow

Below See what I mean about a mirror finish and straight body. Deep black paint is set off with stock stainless side trim and Bel Air badge

Bad '55 Delivery

Above The interior carries on the wild theme, black velour, rolled and pleated over 1980 Corvette seats; boxes behind the front seats hold all those needed things for long journeys, and they have murals on them, seen when flipped up

Right Dan shows the suicide doors. Chevrolet hung the doors the other way round, non suicide. The rear lights are verticle and frenched into the rear fenders. The paint speaks for itself, mural is special if you like 'fat bottomed' girls!

Overleaf With the one piece hood flipped forward, a startling small block Corvette engine is revealed with a gold plated 671 GMC supercharger topped off with two Holley 650s. Everything has been polished, chromed or anodised. Sitting below are many parts from a 1980 Camaro, including a set of disc brakes and steering. A Turbo 400 auto helps turn the '78 Corvette rear axle

Left This is part of a 'His' and 'Her' feature; this is the 'Her' side. I must admit that Karen Craft's '55 210 is one of my favourites. Taillight is a Lee lens, an aftermarket item made in the '50s, with the addition of the bow tie, '55 figures and star. These rear lenses must be on the rare side, the stock '55s have a red lens above the white reversing light

Below 327 cu.in. small block is equipped with modified 270 heads and an ESK cam and Mallory ignition system. Headman headers get rid of the spent gases. The most visible part of the engine is the six Holleys on an Offenhauser manifold, topped with individual chrome air cleaners. Gearbox is the all trusty 3-speed Turbo 350 auto

The interior has the neat
theme too. The
upholstery was by D&F
Upholstery and is done
in red crushed velvet
with gold buttons and
braid as contrast.
Carpets are the same
colour and a neat
finishing touch. Stock
dash with pin striping,
red and white 'tear
drop' knobs for radio
and switches. Steering
is a '67 Pontiac tilt. The
two small toggle
switches, projecting
from the base of the
seat, are for the
hydraulic lifts

Above This '55 sits really low, with the front lowered six inches and the rear five. But wait Karen doesn't have to drive it that low and endanger the underside when grounding out; Ken installed hydraulic lifts all round so that the car can have sufficient ground clearance when required. Ken completed the chassis work and the bodywork, he painted it in '79 Chevy red. Chromestar wires shod with Goodyear radials with raised white letters and Lakes pipes, pinstriping finishes the car in fine style

Overleaf 'His' and 'Hers' together. Karen Craft on the left and Ken Craft on the right, both own '55 210 Chevrolets, far from stock

23

Above Ken's '55 has much more in body modifications than Karen's. He carried out all the bodywork, first chopping the top by four in., lowering the front six in., and the rear five in.; giving low mean look.

The hood is stuffed with louvres and a custom tube grill replaces the stock egg box grill. The hood bird ornament and badge have been removed to clean up the front. Pinstriping and Appleton spotlights give the 'custom' look

Left The rear of Ken's '55 has had the 'custom' treatment with the removal of the badge, key and licence plate, also the little 'V' badges on the end of the fenders if this car had had a V8 in when built in 1955.

Super pinstriping is around the radio aerial and rear lights and to give it a finishing touch, a pair of 1950s aftermarket Lee lenses

Below *Midnite Delite* was a major award winner at the Columbus Classic Chevy Convention. The chop job of four in., gives the car a mean look. No external door handles as the locks work on electric solenoids, vertical trim to the belt line dip has been taken away and Lakes pipes have been installed under door sills. Hydraulic rams have been installed at the front end. Appliance wires with Goodyear radials finish it off.

Under the hood is a similar set up to Karen's; 327 cu.in. Chevy small block Duntof cam, Power Pack heads, Tube headers, Mallory ignition, Offenhauser manifold with six Holley carbs

The black acrylic enamel paint applied by Ken is contrasted beautifully by the blue crushed velvet in a diamond tuft pattern. The front seats are Monte Carlo and they swivel, the rear 'wrap round' back seat is made from Ford T-bird. Stock dash is complemented by '50s 'tear drop' switch knobs, as in Karen's, but black and white. Steering wheel is '67 Cadillac and tilts. Ken has a body shop called Woody's in Centerburg, Ohio

David's '56 Bel Air

Above Also trim is stock '56 to keep the original look. The rear axle is stock '56, but Dave fitted a shackle kit to give the rear some lift, and traction bars to stop some tramp. A pair of Gabriel air shocks have also been fitted to help with rear end stability

Top '56 Chevy seem to be in the minority everywhere, everyhow. David Nicholls from Essex in England owns this fine example, sporting a set of Western Mags with Goodrich tyres. The body is a '56 Bel Air Sport Coupe, pillarless and ideal for cruising in the summer

Right The one external component that is not stock is the hand-operated spotlight which also doubles as a rear-view mirror. Binks of Leytonstone worked on the upholstery, fitting highbacks from an Olds Toronado.

Bussey Motor Services performed on the body and Andrew Styczynski painted it. Neat little sticker tells all

Below David eased in a good rodders' favourite, a high horsepower 327 small block with a Crane cam and Headman headers feeding dual tailpipes. The engine is ex '68 Chevrolet Chevelle SS. An alloy Powerglide takes care of the gear shifting. Steering is power assisted as are the brakes, stock on the rear and discs on the front to help stop this '56 under the influence of the high performance Chevy small block

Big Bopper

Mike Holderman, a welder at General Motors, found his '57 Chevy ten years ago in La Fontaine, his home town in Indiana; the purchase price was a mere $250 dollars. Construction time was nine years which shows in the overall quality. Mike carried out all the work on the car apart from the upholstery. Body modifications are shaved hood and trunk and 198 louvres were punched into the hood!

Dale L. Egle carried out a super job of covering the swivel Monte Carlo bucket seats, door panels, centre custom consul, rear seats and roll around the tilt steering column (topped with a Grant wheel) with maroon crushed velvet in tuck and roll diamond tufted pattern. To complete the interior he used maroon carpets, exactly colour matched to the crushed velvet. Just imagine cruising Bel Air Boulevard with the Alpine AM/FM cassette playing Beach Boys music. Neat interior, Dale; he also has a '57 called *Poison Ivy*

33

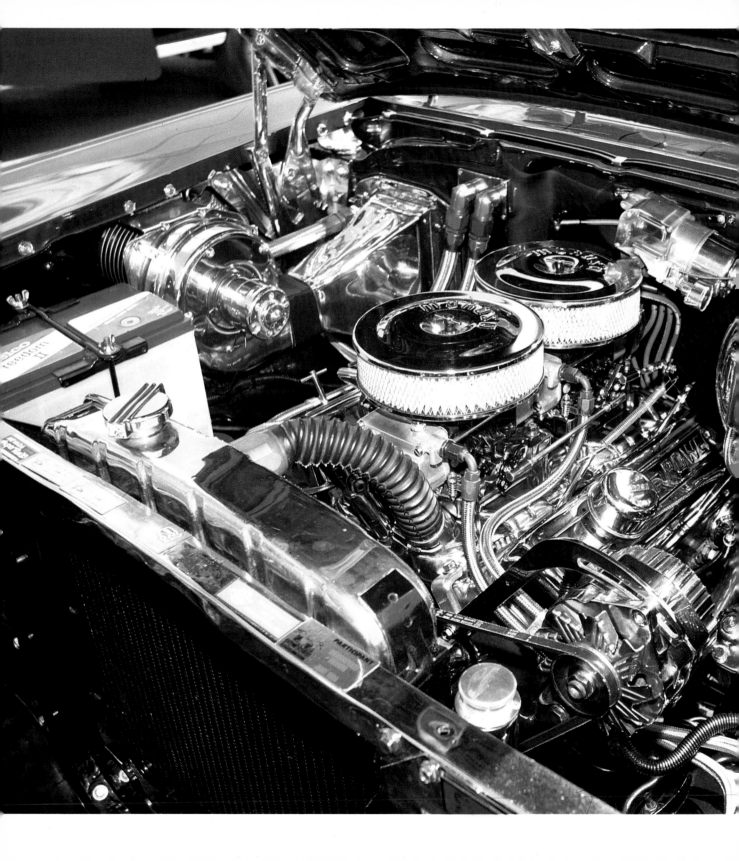

Above Mike is proud of his '57 and rightly so; many hours work and it's never trailered. The rear licence plate has been frenched into the trunk and the door handles are flush type from a Grand Prix. Mike also applied the very striking paint using Candy Brandywine over Gold, Pearl and shadow flames. Neat note on the trunk says 'Baby you know what I like'

Left Neat and immaculate, what other words can describe this '57 engine bay? Hours have been spent getting all the parts in the right place. 350 small block, L46 cam, 327/350 heads, Offenhauser inlet with two Holleys, Black Jack headers playing the V8 burble into Turbo mufflers and just everything is polished or chrome plated. Gearbox is a 350 Turbo with a B&M shift kit

Left An interesting feature of the '57, is that around the headlamp is an air intake fitted to help prolong the life of the fender, keeping down mud and water around this area. And it did work (this was a troublesome area on '55s and '56s in later years). The black rubber bumper guard is an accessory and was not fitted as standard

Above Neat interior of the '57 opposite. Upholstery was carried out by owner Larry Cowgill's wife Cheryl in gold acrylic pile. Other non-stock parts are the Grant woodtrimmed wheel, big and little pedals (big for gas, little for dipper) and walnut gear lever for four on the floor

Above Small block V8 Chevy engines are certainly favourites. This one installed in Larry's '57 is a 302 from a 1968 Z28. A four-barrel pushes in the gas and a GM Hei ignition lights it with Headman tube headers. A Muncie four-speed manual wastes no horsepower, neither does the Positraction 4.11 rear end

Above right Larry Cowgill bought his car from a local Chevy lover so he found the car to be in pretty good condition, but he still stripped it down to the frame. Larry and Cheryl cleaned and repaired where needed and repainted. It took four years to complete, working when they had time. Larry sprayed it with 1970 Cadillac Nottingham Green metallic paint

Right The Positraction rear end is fitted with traction bars to stop axle tramp; wheels are Cragars all round with Goodyear rubber.
   Larry is a Chevrolet dealer (from Caldwell, Ohio) and this shows in his selection of previous cars; '55 Chevy, '57 Chevy Convertible and '59 Chevy

Above The front fender of this '57 Sedan Delivery is covered in louvres – punched not only on the outside but also in the inner fender, in the hood, splash apron, rear tailgate and even in the licence plate. The three louvres punched into the fender fronts are original on the Sedan Delivery, but were just depressions. Dale has capped his with gold anodised aluminium as used on Bel Airs

Right This '57 Sedan Delivery is very rare in Great Britain; the styling of this one is really neat. The side trim was taken from a '57 Bel Air sedan, as the original trim was just a flash from just under the door handle to the end of the fin. Dave loves louvres

Delivery by Dale with Slim's '57

Above The just right stance of Dale's Delivery was achieved by cutting two coils from the stock front suspension. The stock rear suspension is lowered by four in. blocks between the axle and leaf springs. All trim is original '57 from across the range. Wheels are super chrome Weld Wires made with chunky spokes and covered with Eagle Goodyears. Paint is red Lipstick Enamel and is really brilliant in the USA sun. Headlamps are covered with a '50's aftermarket Moons cover. The car was drag raced for six years and held track records, thereafter in storage until eight years ago when Dale started to show it. It was 1982/83 Great Lakes Isca Division Class Champ, Custom Sedan Delivery

Left Standard '57 dash, '64 Chevrolet bucket seats covered with crushed velvet in Diamond Tucked, as are the door panels, head liner and the whole of the rear. Very plush!

Above Dale Watkins cruises around with Martin Coones (Slim) who owns the '57 Hard Top Bel Air, so we thought it would be neat to photograph them together. Slim has owned his since new in 1957 making it a genuine one owner. Lots of custom parts are on the car; Lakes pipes under the door sills, chrome wire wheels with whitewall tyres, fender skirts on the rear. The hood has lots of louvres and has been nosed having the twin lance windsplits removed

Below Everything under the hood is polished chrome or aluminium including the under hood itself. Bumper guard accessories that were in rubber have been turned-up of aluminium and highly polished. The engine is a stock V8 Chevrolet and everything around it or on it has had the chrome treatment – hood catches, radiator, tank, battery cover, heater motor, inner fender panels and more

Tri
Four
Doors

These Continental kits held the spare wheel giving some extra room in the trunk. Martin Coones assured me this is a genuine GM accessory, he bought it himself and fitted it to the '57 in the picture. Not being able to leave anything standard, Martin fitted the gold grill and removed the Chevrolet word badge and centralised the 'V'. He has also doubled up on the rear lights by fitting another light in the bumper where the reversing light was; all tail lights carry blue dots

Above This beautiful example of a '55 four-door Bel Air is outstanding in that all the trim parts are as original, as for the 210 and 150. A bar runs through the top of the bumper overriders and extra bumper guards are fitted

Below Another shot of Al Hudson's immaculate '55 four-door Bel Air shows all the extras including a Continental wheel kit which could be purchased for $123. The two-tone paint was unknown before 1955 and came with the roof only, or roof, upper rear quarter and deck. Al insisted this is an original '55 Chevrolet colour scheme. 1955 saw Chevrolet launch the small block V8 – it was a high performance overhead valve, lightweight engine. In all cars of this year a 'V' badge was fitted on the rear fender between the taillight and bumper

Above The four-door Bel Air was different from the 210 by having trim along the front fender and into the front door, also the Bel Air badge on the rear door. On this super example is a chip guard around the petrol flap. A total of 345, 372 Bel Airs were made; the 210 four door accounted for well over one third of the total cars produced. Two-tone paint is different from Al's by just painting the roof in a different colour

Above right Speeding down the road to the Classic Chevy meeting at the Hilton East Hotel in Columbus, is a Bel Air Hard Top, four door. When both front and rear windows are rolled down you turn it into a pillarless car. 133,670 of this model were sold

Right The plaque in the window proclaimed: Original-unrestored, Original paint, Original interior, Original chrome. Owner Frank and Vickie Orlando, Waynesburg, Ohio. 1957 four-door Sedan. What more can we say!

Rag Tops

If you had wanted to buy this '55 Chevrolet Convertible in 1955 it would have cost you $2305. Wonder how much Jim Moonan would take for this all black paint with white roof now? Extra trim parts from fender down the door sill, extra bumper guards, wire wheel covers are not original '55 Chevrolet

The Bel Air Convertible was chosen in 1955 to be the
Indy 500 pace car. With the high performance V8
installed it was a good choice but this convertible is not
claiming to be that car, although it does have a V8
engine according to the 'V' trim on the rear fender. Ernie
Chauvin travelled down from Ontario, Canada in his
restored '55 two-door Bel Air Convertible

Right A note of explanation was attached to the side of this '56 Convertible Bel Air. It explains; this '55 Chevy was used in accident scenes filmed in the movie *Heart and Soul* filmed in Pickaway County and various parts of Ohio. Owned by Jim Le Masters. With relatively few Convertibles made, I hope the film company paid to have it restored to original specification

Below All Convertibles were under the Bel Air series for the years '55, '56 and '57, and in 1956 just over 41,000 Convertibles were made. Two-tone paint is nicely split by the side trim

Above Cecil Hall's '56 Convertible is as stock as they come, right down to wheels being of the correct pattern. The car was driven down from Canada to Columbus, Ohio. It was also equipped with a full Continental kit.

Cecil, his wife and poodle enjoyed cruising around. I am sure I saw the poodle drive at least once over the weekend

Above The Bel Air Convertible was not only produced in two-tone colours but also in solid; this example is in solid black with a white roof. If you look carefully at any '56 there does not appear to be a flap or door to gain access to the gas tank, the rear taillight on the offside of the car (American) hinges back to reveal the filler cap

Right The '57 rear was completely redesigned. Fins now appeared and taillights at the base of the fin

The '55 Convertible in front started the Tri-Chevy craze and the '57 behind was the end, only one year apart, but the styling was light years away. The '57 solid red, with red and grey interior, is owned by Frank Hartmen and looks long and sleek, the '55 looks short and stocky by comparison, but the wheelbase is 115 in., on both cars. Overall length of the '55 is 195.6 in., the '57 200

Two Door Tri

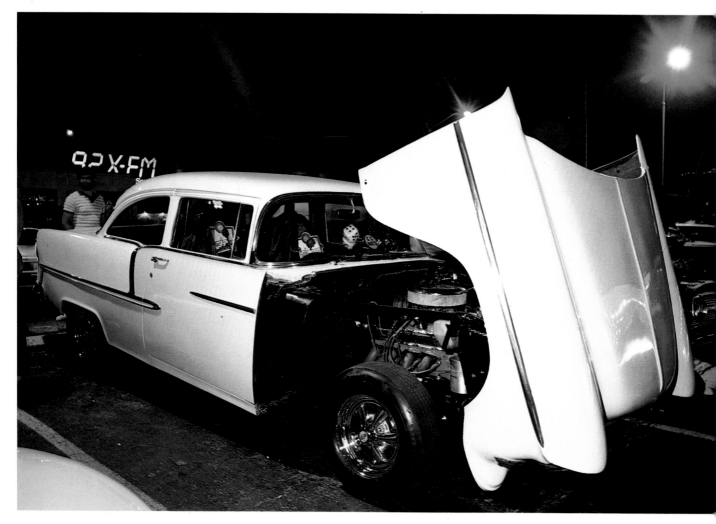

Above While cruising Jerry's Drive-in in Columbus, Ohio on a Friday evening, I was tempted to shoot this two-door '55. Fibreglass tilt front is readily available in the USA for all years of Tri-Chevys and is priced around $400. This car is equipped with a big block Chevy of 400 cu.in. or more, Holley and tube headers; must be a quick car

Above right This '55 was fairly heavily customised, the body has had the rear trim removed, the radio aerial has been frenched and the rear lights have the '55 chrome bezel, but the lenses have been removed. The rear wheel arch is drastic

Right 1955 210 sedan in full flight. The '55 rear wheelarch is flat and the '56 is tear drop in shape

Left '55 Bel Air complete with front fender side trim, rear fender trim, gas cap trim and lower stoneguard from wheelarch along door sill and, of course, cruising would not be complete with out the fuzzy dice

Below Says Bel Air on the side above the rear fender trim but Bel Air's should have front fender trim. Two other identification points – '55s have an egg box grill which is more elongated on the '56, '55 side lights are lip shaped while '56 are square. Nice clean car with chrome wire wheels

Right Steve Best's *High and Mighty* high ridin' two-tone paint '55 Bel Air is in a style of a few years back when Tris were jacked sky high. The way this height is achieved is by fitting the rear leaf springs on top of the axle instead of the usual place slung under. This Chevy was lifted at the front by modified stub axles too. Steve also loaded in a 396 big block Chevy V8 to give plenty of go

Far right Supercharger whine coming from John Javert's white '55. After John has passed you are left with only the fading heavy beat of a mighty V8

Below Smoothed out front with tube grill in place of the egg box, hood bird and badge have gone and lots of louvres have been punched in the hood of this '55 Bel Air sedan

Above Around 185,000 Bel Air Sport Coupes were produced in 1955. The number plate shows what this owner thinks of his car

Below You don't see many Tris with big blocks but this '55 two-door Hard Top not only runs a 427 cu.in. V8 Chevy engine but Steve Grant decided he would pump even more into it by fitting a Dyers 671 supercharger with ten per cent overdrive. Eight Venolia low compression pistons, Fireball 300 Crane cam and Carter 750CFM all help. All this gas in the chamber is fired by a Mallory ignition system. Gearbox is GM Turbo 400 with B&M Quickshift modifications. The rear axle is a 12-bolt Positive Traction unit to take all the horsepower

Overleaf Can you believe that this '56 Bel Air two-door Hard Top has only 25,000 miles on the clock and that's in 28 years of motoring? We were able to find David Reid who owns this '56. He has had the car since 1976, it has the original 265 cu.in. engine which because of the 25,000 has only just been 'run in'. The whole car is original

Left Night photography has always been my favourite; warm Ohio July evening, tripod, plenty of background lighting and my faithful Mecablitze 502 flash, and some really neat cars like Mike's 1956 Bel Air two-door Sports Coupe. It's in a super two-tone blue paint. Could have been my car with that licence plate!

Below left The driver of this '56 drag racer could have been either Mr Kincaid or Mr Hartman. He was driving from a Friday night meet to a Saturday night meet and was passing close to the Classic Chevy Convention so he decided to call in. We did gather that the car travelled the quarter mile in 12.80 sec. and finished at 106 mph. The engine is the ever excellent 350 with a centre squirt carburettor

Above Look over this page at the racer and then at this '56 210 and you can see the difference between it and Bel Air trim

Right Several things confuse the '55 and '56. This two-door Bel Air has a perfect hood bird with 'V' and badge. No 'V' on the '55 and a different bird

Below Unusual it certainly is. Ok, it looks like it's been jacked up with suspension mods, but no this '56 (sorry, it's a four-door) has been removed from the original chassis and placed on a four wheel drive chassis which certainly lifts it up compared with that '57 Bel Air Sports Coupe (yes, it's a two-door) sitting beside it

'57s are completely different from '55s and '56s. At the rear we have a pair of finned fenders, just above the rear taillight and in the tail fin, driver's side, the gas cap is hidden. This '57 Bel Air two-door Sports Coupe is owned by Gene Rishforth and is one of the most collectable models today

Above One way to get your Tri-Chevy to a meet is to pop it on a trailer. Larry decided that this was the way to go with his '57. Personally I have only trailered one of my cars to a show over the past ten years. This was my '32 Ford when it had low oil pressure. I like to drive my street rods, as I get a kick out of driving as well as showing. One cannot criticise trailering as one does not know the situation the car is in – not street legal, etc. This is a nice car and is in our gallery section

Left This '57 Bel Air Sports Coupe was outside Cleveland. We stopped and took a look at the car. Asking price was $2200 (original price as $2399 in 1957) for an exterior not in bad shape but the interior had been messed about and was tatty. Write to us for the telephone number!

Above Continental kit exposed on this '57. Putting the spare tyre outside the trunk obviously gives you more inside

Left Martin, Slim to his friends, cruises a Columbus highway in his custom '57 which he purchased in March 1957 new and equipped it with the hottest engine at that time, a 283 V8 with big valves and four barrel. Slim is retired now, loves his '57 and tells me it has only had snow on the car once. Just pulling into the picture is Dale in his '57 Sedan Delivery

Above '57 Bel Air under power. Good looking Sports Coupe's lines are so good, it looks as if it is flying down the road even when it's standing still

Right The trunk is shaved (Chevy badge and large 'V' taken off) on Dale Egle's '57 210 Sedan and is named *Poison Ivy*. Organic green candy apple over black pearl paint. Super pinstriping too. Dale and his wife are two neat people and the car is one of the best

Above The side trim varies on '57s. The 150 has a
horizontal bar along the rear fender and vertical to the
belt line dip but we could not find this model at the
Classic Chevy Convention. The 210 and Bel Air have trim
as you see in this photo, 210's have the forward pointing
'triangle' painted on two-tone paint schemes with the
second colour, obviously on a solid colour car it was
painted with the same colour. On the Bel Air, Harley Earl
designed a brushed aluminium panel with the Bel Air
badge in gold

Nomad and Delivery

Above This 1956 Chevy Sedan Delivery was of very high quality but we could not find the owner to get more information. It is an excellent example, possibly the second Delivery the guy has built, and runs a blower under the air intake and dual Holley carbs

Left '55 two-door Wagon turned up for sale on a low loader at Columbus. Cost when new was $2178, wonder how much this primed beauty went for? Wagons and Sedan Deliveries are without a belt line dip

Below Nomads are really in a class of their own. This custom '55 is a fine example, candy red paint and pinstriped flames. The front trim parts are all true '55. The wheelarch is cut much more into the body, trim across the front lights and down the fender sides was different from other '55s and called an 'eyebrow'. The sill trim was optional on the '55 Nomad

Above Line up goes '55 Wagon, '55 Wagon, '56 Nomad. All Nomads had vertical trims on the rear tailgate. The whole rear end had a more slanted appearance than the Wagons

Left All Nomads were Bel Airs. This sparkling example, owned by Robert Sykona, was a newly restored car, he was fitting the windscreen at midnight, the night before the Classic Chevy weekend. No wonder these Nomads are sought after, with only 8530 cars built in 1955. They are particularly pretty and ultra rare in England. It's amazing that something so good-looking sold so badly. *Motor Trend* in late '55 gave it third place in their 'Most aesthetically styled' contest for '55, with Chrysler and Ford in front

Overleaf I just had to stop and shoot this picture of a Nomad '55 filling up with gas. Taillights are stock '55, Nomad script appears above the centre trim in the tailgate, seven trims in all. All years had seven and all years had the script. 'V' badges on the '55 would not fit the '56 and vice versa as the fenders on the '55 were a different shape. These badges signified V8 engines were fitted. The rear bumpers were the same as '55 Wagons

Above left High riding '56 Nomad. A straight axle at the front with leaf springs gives the lift; leaf springs at the rear are a top of the axle, tall tyres at the rear also help in the lift. The side trim helps dramatically with the two-tone paint. The trim at the door pillar was reversed to angle with the pillar

Left Black, straight and a set of polished Centre Lines makes one very sharp '56 Sedan Delivery, owned by Kirk Christensen

Above '57 Nomads were trimmed the same as the Bel Air with brushed aluminium in the 'triangle', gold capped front fender louvres, the ribbed roof was common to all three Nomad models, the only special exterior trim was the Nomad script on the tailgate and a small gold 'V' on V8 powered models. Few of 'The Wagon with the Sports Car Flair' were sold in 1957

1957 Sedan Delivery 150. This very neat Delivery was smooth in its lines, the back being more upright than the Nomad of that year. Less than 10,000 were produced

Tri UK

Above Bob Holland likes to drag race his '55 150. He set about cutting down the weight of the car by fitting a repro fibreglass tilt front but it retains all the original trim. The race theme is carried by the dechromed side trim and radiused rear wheelarches. Fitting tight to the body are five spoke A/R S200 wheels with fat rubber. Installed is a high comp 327 with 650 double pumper Holleys on their 300-2 ally inlet manifold, MSDGA ignition and a bunch of headers plus a Muncie M22 manual gearbox

Above Duncan and Paula also like them hot! Their '55
Bel Air was built to boil the hides on a 12-bolt Posi rear
from a Chevelle. This picture was shot at Gary's Picnic,
Santa Pod Raceway with Duncan at the controls. Race
trim means no front bumper and glass tilt front. The 360
cu.in. was carefully assembled with all-good parts; Crane
cam, Racer Brown springs, big valve heads, Z28 ally high
rise, 750 Holley, Accel ignition and headers. The body
was also worked over by Duncan with help by Les
Harrison and was given a coat of chrome yellow acrylic.
Gone Bananas is the right name for this car!

Above Dead '56 210 four-door Sedan, never to pound the streets again. This 'rotten' photograph was shot at Priors of Yaxham in Norfolk, England

Right A fine example of a 1956 150 rebuilt by Martin West of Brentford with all original trim apart from the side trim which should continue from the vertical belt line dip to the rear bumper. A stock 350 Chevy was installed apart from a Holley carb and headers, Hayes clutch to keep contact between the 350 and Muncie four-speed manual. A set of sparkling chrome Cragar S/S wheels of 6 × 14 front, 7 × 15 rear, contrast well with the black paint. Other goodies help the ride – with Gabriel air shocks and traction bars on the rear and Red Ride shocks on the front. Cherry Bombs hold that lovely V8 burble

Above Rotted out '55 210, two-door Wagon. Not much hope for this car. Great shame to see these cars wasted. Photo taken by kind permission of Priors of Yaxham, Norfolk, England

Left This '56 Chevy Sedan Delivery was bought for £70 sterling in Denmark over four years ago by Jens Fredholm who did not know what he had bought till he saw one similar in an American hot rod magazine! The body was taken off and the chassis completely renovated; a '69 350 small block with 255 horsepower was installed and Turbo 350 auto box. At Gary's Picnic a best time of 15.24 sec. was recorded over a quarter mile after this photo was taken. Body should soon be painted

95

Let's face it, all models of
Tri-Chevy are rare in
England, but convertibles
are on the rare, rare side.
This example owned by
Kevin Collier is just about
how it rolled out of the
GM factory in 1957. It
runs a 283 cu.in. with a
Holley 600CFM, which
helps the mileage, and a
set of headers into a pair
of Cherry Bombs. Two-
speed Powerglide auto
runs the stock rear end
aided by a pair of air
shocks. The interior has
been re-upholstered in red
and white in keeping with
the red paint

Black and flames is
always a sign of a hot
rod. Simon Davies' 1957
150 has all the classic
signs with deep black
paint with orange, white
and red flames,
pinstriping in white and a
set of American racing
wheels, five spoke with
spinners. Under the hood
is the first choice, a 327
backed up by a Turbo
400 running through to
the original rear axle,
supported by leaf springs
and air shocks. A pair of
'69 Camaro discs are in
front to bring up the
braking efficiency. Interior
has been re-upholstered
in deep buttoned, brilliant
wine red dralon

Engines 6 and 8

Left Silver metallic paint on this '57 Bel Air Sports Coupe gives an original look, even down to a set of original wheels with 215-70-14 tyres. A Chevy 350 with a 350 Turbo from a '71 Chevy helps turn those wheels, the engine is just cleaned-up with M/T rocker covers and chrome air cleaner. All the brakes and running gear are stock and that's how Dave Hartshorne wants it, now wanting only to add whitewalls

Below left Two-tone paint, a little different. Harry Blunden owns this super '57 four-door Bel Air. Most of the running gear is all original as are all the trim parts. A small block has been equipped with a Holley, Edelbrock inlet and Black jack headers with Cherry Bomb mufflers

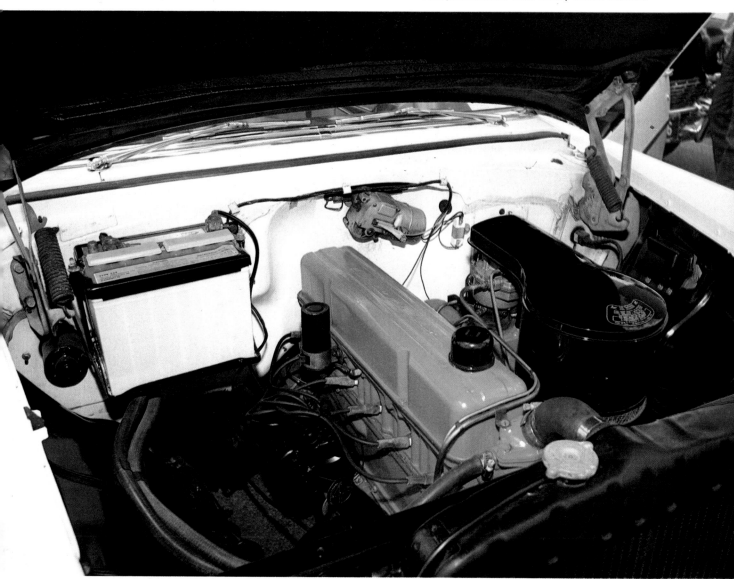

Above 235 cu.in. six in Ruth Anderson's unrestored '56. This is as stock as they come. 125 hp at 4000 rpm with a single barrel and three speed Powerglide

Take your basic 235
cu.in. six cylinder, bolt on
dual carbs, hot cam,
balance, blueprint and
you have a hot little
mover. Then drop it into,
say, a '55 Bel Air, add
dual pipes. Then go
racing

Heaving a 396 Turbo Jet V8
into a '55 is no easy job. The
physical size of this engine is a
problem compared to the small
block Chevy. Cooling the big
block is another problem,
exiting the exhaust gases is
another, and creating all this
power means beefing up the
gearbox plus running a much
stronger rear axle. Life is never
easy in the fast lane

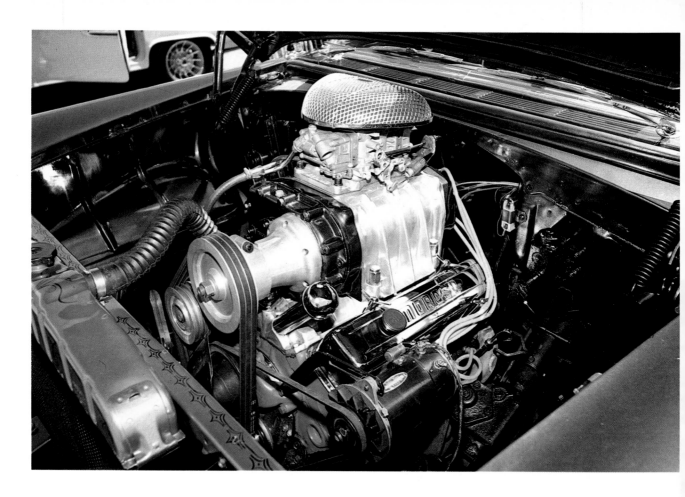

Above Another way to build
up horsepower is to bolt on a
supercharger, and this is just
what James Harting did with
the small block in his '55.
Depending on belt and gear
system you can easily achieve
the familiar whine associated
with a blown engine

Right Here is one at last, a
little old small block. This 265
in David Reid's '56 is as
original as you will see with
only 25,000 miles on it. The
small block from 265 through
350 is such a neat design. All
can be fitted with a variety of
gearboxes. Long live the small
block!

Below Chevy brought out its fuel injection on the 283 V8 in 1957. This example resides in Jay Avner's '57 Convertible. Billed by Chevrolet, in a choice of 250 hp or 283 hp, as the Ram Jet, its fuel injection was built by Rochester but almost entirely designed by GM Engineering. It is said to have better fuel economy, better start and warm up in the cold and providing five horsepower more than twin four barrel carbs

'55 called *Blue Shark* is
heavy in 'custom'; highly
polished engine, lots of
details on the inner
fenders and mural on the
inside of the hood
depicting a tropical scene
to create the name

Interiors by Tri

Blue Shark also provided this example of a swivel seat and velour buttoned interior. Charles Cunningham built and owns the car. Steering wheel cover is removed for driving!

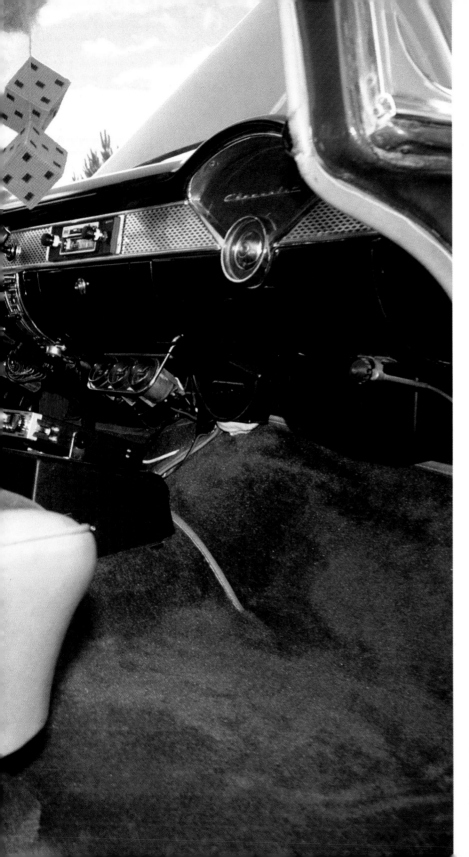

1955 Chevy Sedan dash. The basic
design was used in all models 150,
210 and Bel Air, but this slightly
customised interior includes extra
gauges, radio cassette, CB and tilt
steering column and, of course, a
set of fluffy dice

Different side of a '55 dash.
Notice the double hump, the
housing of speedo in the hump
behind the steering wheel and
Bel Air badge and clock in the
other. Two extra gauges and
rev counter and steering wheel
are non stock and it does have
a nice Chevy flag badge in the
horn button. Stamped in the
aluminium trim running through
the centre of the dash are 987
'bow ties' the official logo of

Above This is as stock as you will see. Cecil Hall's '56 Convertible has a dash with double hump laid out similar way to the '55, quite different are that the 'bow ties' have been swapped for an oblong design

Both left Two neat rear end interiors. The '55 trunk (above) shows off a non stock wheel cover and flares, perhaps to gain points in concours judging. 'Wagon' is equally clean and, of course, isn't stock

Above Here we see the other side of an original '56 dash, with central glove compartment and original design seat cloth and vinyl trim. David Reid owns this fine example

Right The dash design was completely altered for '57. Instruments are now clustered around the speedo, and lights are used for oil and amps. The dash still houses the central glove compartment. Steering wheel is also original, spot light rear-view mirror is an aftermarket accessory and can be adjusted from inside the car. This '57 is owned by Cindy and Dick Brown

Neat Features

Judges at the Convention give this
'55 Chevrolet the once over.
Quality black paint shows with
mirror reflection. Chrome wire
wheels are by Appliance

Above Pinstriping is often used to accentuate parts of the car. This aftermarket accessory mirror is on Karen Craft's 1955 'Low Rider'

Left Holley carbs chrome plated on top of a supercharger out above the hood of *Tempted Twice* a '56 Chevrolet Sedan Delivery. '56 hood bird differs from the '55 design. The Chevrolet emblem over a wide 'V' was on V8s, a larger emblem alone on sixes

Distinctive twin lance windsplits came on all models of 1957 Chevrolet as hood ornaments